A DAY *in the* LIFE *of*
A WORLD WAR II EVACUEE

Alan Childs
Illustrated by Adam Hook

HODDER
Wayland

imprint of Hodder Children's Books

A Day in the Life

Titles in the series

A Roman Centurion
A Tudor Criminal
A Victorian Street Seller
A World War II Evacuee

Editor: Jason Hook
Designer: Jan Sterling
Picture Research: Shelley Noronha

First published in 1999 by Wayland (Publishers) Ltd

Reprinted in 2002 by Hodder Wayland,
an imprint of Hodder Children's Books

© Hodder Wayland 1999

British Library Cataloguing in Publication Data
Childs, Alan,
   A day in the life of a World War II evacuee
   1. World War, 1939-1945 – Great Britain – Evacuation of civilians – Juvenile
   literature 2. Great Britain – Social life and customs – 1939-1945 – Juvenile
   literature 3. Great Britain – Rural conditions – 20th century – Juvenile literature
   I. Title
   941'.084

   ISBN 0 7502 2676 5

Printed in Hong Kong

Cover picture: (foreground) the evacuee; (background) *London during dockland air raids*, painted in 1941 by Charles Pears.

Picture Acknowledgements: The publishers would like to thank the following for permission to publish their pictures: Alan Childs 29 (bottom); Bridgeman Art Library, London, /Guildhall Art Gallery, Corporation of London *cover*; Camera Press 23 (bottom); Hulton Getty 6 (left), 9 (top), 10 (bottom), 11 (bottom), 24 (left), 25 (bottom), 27 (top), 29 (top); Imperial War Museum, London 4, 19 (top), 23 (top); John Frost Historical Newspapers 22 (top); Museum of London 12 (top); Peter Newark 20, 28 (top); Popperfoto 6 (right), 7 (bottom); Public Record Office 5 (bottom), 15 (bottom); Robert Opie 8 (top), 25 (top), 26; Ronald Grant Archive 24 (right); Science and Society Picture Library 5 (top), 7 (top), 9 (bottom), 11 (top-left), 18 (left), 19 (bottom), 21 (top), 22 (bottom); Topham 13, 14, 15 (top), 21 (bottom), 27 (bottom), 28 (bottom); Wayland Picture Library 10 (top), 11 (centre), 18 (right).

All Wayland books encourage children to read and help them improve their literacy.

✓ The contents page, page numbers, headings and index help locate specific pieces of information.

✓ The glossary reinforces alphabetic knowledge and extends vocabulary.

✓ The further information section suggests other books dealing with the same subject.

✓ Find out more about how this book is specifically relevant to the National Literacy Strategy on page 31.

CONTENTS

The Evacuees	4
Billets and Hosts	6
School	8
Gas Masks	10
Air Raids	12
Rations	14
New Arrivals	16
The 'Cattle Market'	18
'Dig for Victory'	20
'Careless Talk'	22
At the Pictures	24
Home Guard	26
Fun in Wartime	28
Glossary & Books to Read	30
Literacy Information	30
Timeline & Sources of Quotes	31
Index	32

Meet our evacuee, Mary. She is eleven years old, and feeling very nervous. It is 1940, and she has been sent away from London, with her little brother Tommy, to a safer place in the countryside. Like a parcel, she has been labelled, and is now about to meet 'Granny' and 'Grandpa' Robertson, her host family. She carries her favourite teddy, and her gas mask is round her neck. Her other belongings are packed in her dad's old leather suitcase. Mary does not know when she will see her mum again. She hopes desperately that her new family will be kind to her.

The candle-clock that appears on each spread is a way of telling the time which was invented over a thousand years ago. It takes an hour for each ring of wax to burn down, as you will see.

THE EVACUEES

Even after a night's sleep, Mary feels exhausted. She wakes her brother, and they sit together in their strange new bedroom, staring at their few possessions. Mary remembers the tears as her mum packed the suitcase yesterday morning. Then she thinks of last night, when she nervously met her new family for the first time.

When the Second World War began in 1939, millions of children were evacuated to the countryside, away from British cities that were in danger of being bombed by German aircraft. Brothers and sisters were usually evacuated together. Even so, it must have been terrifying to leave your family behind and begin a new life far from home.

◀ Evacuees like Mary left their homes and went to live with 'host families'. Some evacuees stayed for six years.

▶ Two evacuees with their bags and identity labels.

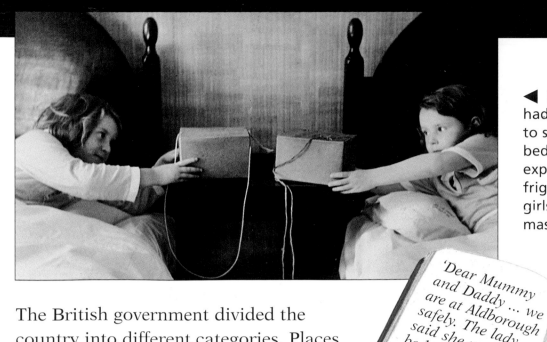

◀ Evacuees who had a brother or sister to share their new bedroom, found their experience a little less frightening. These girls keep their gas masks at their bedside.

The British government divided the country into different categories. Places that might be bombed, such as cities and ports, were called 'evacuable areas'. Places in the countryside, where it was thought children would be safer, were called 'reception areas'. Parents were urged to send their children to reception areas, but they were not forced to do so.

'Dear Mummy and Daddy … we are at Aldborough safely. The lady said she would be kind to us … there is a lovely village green. Mrs Norman lives in the country … The first night we slept in a stable in a racecourse.' [1]

[Turn to page 31 to see who wrote the quotes in this book.]

Millions of children were evacuated during the first three days of September 1939. Many of them returned home after a short time, because the German bombing had not started. The government put up posters to persuade parents to leave their children in reception areas. But many families were so unhappy at being separated that they brought their children home. A year later, the bombing of London finally began. Now many more children had to be evacuated.

CHILDREN
are safer in the country
. . . leave them there

◀ The government used pictures of smiling children on posters like this one to try to show worried parents that evacuees were happy.

BILLETS AND HOSTS

Tommy sits in front of the breakfast table, while Granny Robertson combs her fingers through his hair. 'Just checking for nits,' she says, 'The last 'vaccies we had were crawling with them.' Mary watches in horror as the old lady takes a pair of scissors and begins cutting off her brother's hair.

Evacuees often received quite a shock when they first arrived at their new home or 'billet'. Their new parents, or 'hosts', were worried that evacuees would bring head lice and a skin disease called impetigo into their home. So, some poor evacuees were welcomed by being plunged into a bath and having their heads shaved.

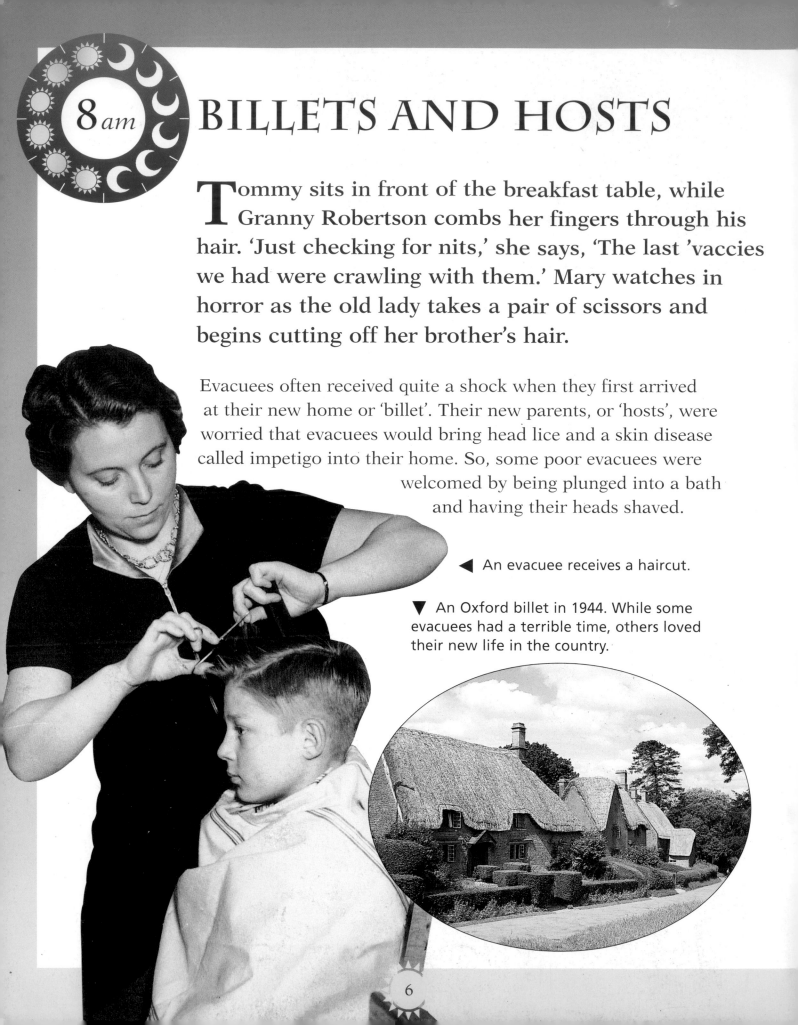

◀ An evacuee receives a haircut.

▼ An Oxford billet in 1944. While some evacuees had a terrible time, others loved their new life in the country.

◄ These children are waiting to be given their cod liver oil. This helped to make strong bones, and prevent a disease called rickets, but it tasted horrible.

'I had a boy of eleven in my class whose foster mother complained that he was wetting the bed ... one of our welfare workers went round to the house, and found that to get to the lavatory at night this boy had to go through his foster parents' bedroom. And he had no chamber pot.' [2]

Many frightened evacuees suffered from bed-wetting. Hosts who grew angry about this problem simply made it worse. Host families were responsible for the health of children in their care, and evacuees had to queue up for regular doses of foul-tasting cod liver oil.

Some evacuees from poor homes had proper bathrooms for the first time. But during wartime, hot water was rationed. Baths were meant to contain no more than five inches (12.5 cm) of water, and a line was often painted around the side of the bath at this height.

◄ Evacuees being bathed in a school in Windsor, 1941.

9 am SCHOOL

Mary's stomach feels full of butterflies, as she sees her new school for the first time. She stands outside the iron railings until one of her old friends from home spots her. Together, they walk slowly into the playground. All the evacuees stand in one corner, and all the locals in another. Some of the village children are calling them names.

▲ School equipment was scarce, because of war shortages.

Schools somehow had to squeeze in their normal pupils as well as a large number of evacuees. Some classes contained as many as seventy children, and equipment was in very short supply. Teachers checked exercise books regularly to make sure that children were not wasting paper, and some pupils even had to share pencils.

Many teachers were quite old. They had come out of retirement to replace younger teachers who had gone away to serve with the armed forces. These younger teachers often came to visit their old pupils, dressed in their smart new army, navy or air-force uniforms.

◄ A teacher gives a lesson about air raids, using a scrap of metal taken from a crashed German aeroplane.

▶ These evacuees from London are being taught in Lacock Abbey, a country house in Wiltshire, in 1939.

In some schools, local children were taught in the morning and evacuees in the afternoon. While one group was using the classrooms, the other might have games or a nature ramble. Some evacuees were taught outdoors or in grand country houses. One girl who had her lessons in Lacock Abbey remembered: 'Going to the 'lav' was particularly scary; it was situated in the crypt below the abbey.'

In school playgrounds, fights often broke out between local children and the evacuees. Sometimes even the parents of local children taunted the 'dirty 'vaccies'. Evacuees were resented because of overcrowding, and because many of them looked and sounded so different. But there was also plenty of excitement for evacuees at school. Lessons were interrupted for air-raid drills, and collections were made for causes like the Spitfire Fund, which raised money to build more aeroplanes.

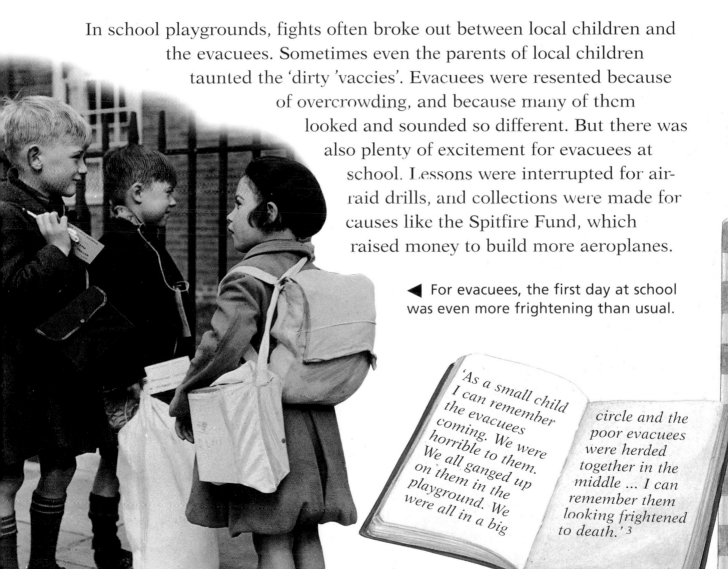

◀ For evacuees, the first day at school was even more frightening than usual.

'As a small child I can remember the evacuees coming. We were horrible to them. We all ganged up on them in the playground. We were all in a big circle and the poor evacuees were herded together in the middle ... I can remember them looking frightened to death.' [3]

GAS MASKS

The teacher stops the lesson, and announces: 'We are going to practise working in our gas masks. Get them out of their boxes please.' The children groan and Mary's heart sinks. She hates the horrible mask with its suffocating feeling and rubbery smell. In her old school, they had to keep them on for ages.

▲ Children loved making rude noises with 'Mickey Mouse' masks like this one.

Because it was feared that German aeroplanes would drop bombs that contained poisonous gas, everyone was given a gas mask. Children under five had a 'Mickey Mouse' mask, with bright colours to make them want to wear it. Babies were put inside a much larger device, into which air was pumped. There were even gas-proof prams. Air-raid wardens had gas masks with long hoses reaching to a 'speaking box' on their belts, through which they could shout instructions.

◀ A mother with her baby and his special gas mask, in 1940.

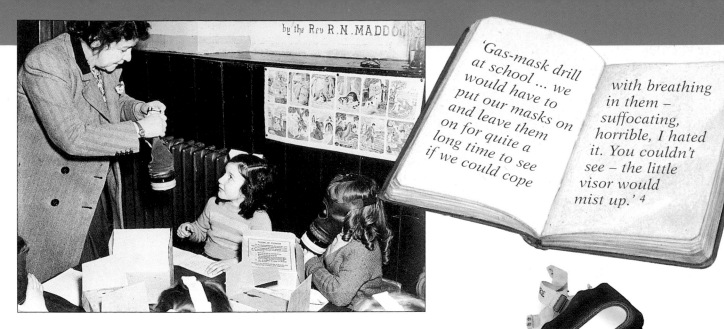

'Gas-mask drill at school ... we would have to put our masks on and leave them on for quite a long time to see if we could cope with breathing in them – suffocating, horrible, I hated it. You couldn't see – the little visor would mist up.' [4]

▲ A teacher helps her pupils to put on their gas masks.

Children in school quickly learnt how to put on their gas masks and work with them on. It was very difficult to speak in them, and the little glass windows soon misted up. The bottom of the mask contained charcoal to filter poison out of the air.

At the beginning of the war, people took great care of their gas masks and took them everywhere. Some even had decorated cases made for them. But as time passed, and no gas attacks came, people stopped carrying their masks. By the end of the war, many masks had been left in attics.

▲ An adult's gas mask.

▼ A gas-mask practice in 1941.

11am AIR RAIDS

'Run rabbit, run rabbit, run, run, run.' It is mid-morning, and Mary and the other children sing as they sit crushed together in the school air-raid shelter. As the last moans of the air-raid siren fade away, the warden calls out the register. Someone whispers that a German plane has passed over the village, with its engine on fire.

▲ A fire-watcher's helmet, axe, logbook and badge. On the right is a German incendiary bomb.

Even in the countryside, there were air raids. German aeroplanes, flying home after bombing cities such as London, would drop their remaining bombs before they reached the coast. When the wailing siren sounded, air-raid wardens made sure that everyone was under cover. Volunteers called 'fire-watchers' kept a lookout in case bombs set light to buildings.

◀ The air-raid warden blew a whistle to signal an air raid, or used a rattle to signal a gas drill.

'There hadn't been any sirens for a while and the shelters were full of water and frogs, and the boys were catching the frogs and putting them down the girls' necks ... We had four more sirens that day, and each time my class were first out and last back.' 5

◄ An air-raid warden and teachers check that every child is safely in a shelter, in 1939. It was this school's first air-raid practice of the war.

Schools had their own shelters, which in some places were dug out under the playground. There were regular practices to make sure that children could get to them in a hurry. At home, many people built an Anderson shelter in their garden. Other people sheltered inside their homes, either in steel cages called Morrison shelters or underneath the stairs.

Some pupils manned their school's air-raid siren. Schoolchildren also took it in turns to watch out for enemy aeroplanes. They could recognize their shapes, and even the different engine noises, so they could tell if it was a German aeroplane or 'one of ours'. It was a frightening time, but very exciting as well.

▼ Children examine the crater in the middle of their school playground, caused by a German bomb.

12 pm RATIONS

With their stomachs rumbling, Tommy and Mary queue up with Granny at the grocer's. It is a long wait before the woman can finally serve them. 'We have to get your ration books registered here,' Granny tells them, 'So that you can get your fair share of food. We've also got fresh vegetables from the allotment for dinner tonight.'

Food became scarce during the war, because German submarines sunk many ships carrying supplies to Britain. Rationing was introduced, which meant that people were only allowed to buy small amounts of certain foods. Brown ration books were issued for adults, blue for children, and green for expectant mums and babies. Shop assistants marked or cut out the coupons in a ration book, to show that a shopper had received their weekly ration.

◀ A shop assistant cuts out the coupons from a ration book. Oranges were reserved for children and expectant mums.

▼ Bacon, butter, cheese, tea, sugar, jam and sweets were all rationed during the war.

ORANGES FOR CHILDREN ONLY

► These ladies are waiting in the snow for the shops to open. They had to queue early if they wanted to make certain of receiving enough food for their families.

'The food queues seemed to stretch for miles. I remember one of my friends always had money in her purse, because her mother used to say: "Now if you see a queue on the avenue, you've got to get in it, just buy whatever it is. Here's half a crown (12½p)."' 6

Mums and grannies became used to queuing for food. They also invented many strange recipes, to use what food was available. Children noticed carrots in almost everything – from carrot cookies to carrot jam. Tinned spam became popular in the war, and people also ate fried whalemeat.

It was important not to waste food in wartime. Scraps were saved and fed to pigs. People also joined 'pig clubs', where they helped to feed a pig in exchange for a share of its meat. Pig bins were placed on street corners for people to throw in their scraps. Useful recipes were also broadcast on the wireless to help people prepare attractive meals from unusual cuts of meat, such as trotters and brains.

SAVE KITCHEN WASTE TO FEED THE PIGS!

THANKS

KEEP IT DRY, FREE FROM GLASS, METAL, BONES, PAPER ETC.

KITCHEN WASTE

IT ALSO FEEDS POULTRY ···*Your Council will collect*

◄ Posters reminded everyone that feeding scraps to pigs would help provide more food.

NEW ARRIVALS

As the church clock strikes one, Mary watches a new party of evacuees arrive. They stumble wearily out of the station doorway. She knows just how they feel. A billeting officer shouts: 'You will now be taken to the village hall, to be chosen by your new families.'

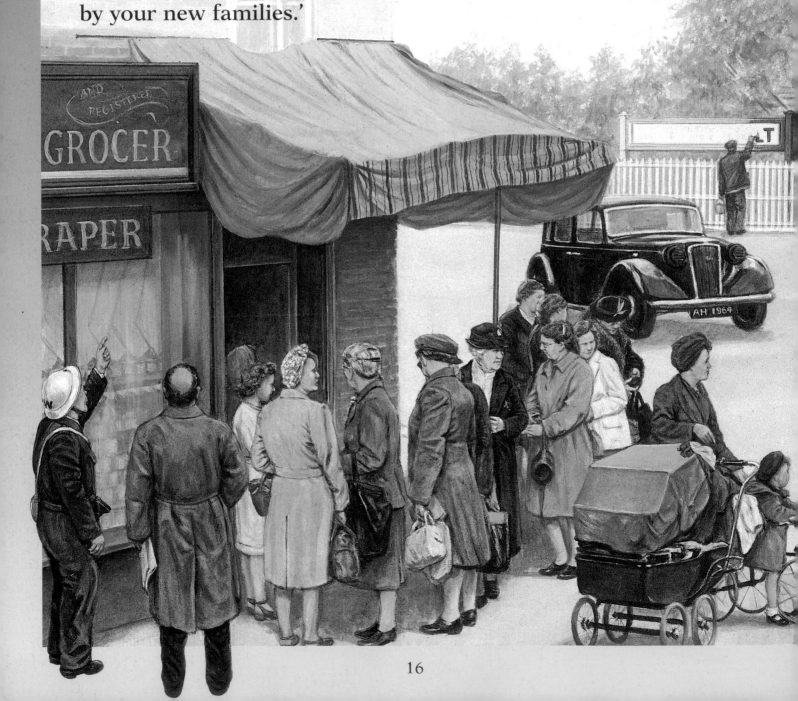

Women queuing for food rations watch as evacuees and their teachers arrive in the village. Can you spot the five characters who appear elsewhere in this book? How many things can you see which show us that it is wartime? You can find out more on page 31.

THE 'CATTLE MARKET'

In the village hall, local families choose their evacuees. Friends hold hands tightly, anxiously hoping they will not be separated. The tidy, quiet children seem to be chosen first. As the room empties, those still left turn their eyes to the ground. It is like a cattle market at which they have not been bought.

▼ Evacuees with their labels and bags in 1940.

One of the worst parts of evacuation day for many children was waiting to be chosen by a host family. Sometimes, their homes had already been chosen and they were simply taken to them. But in other places, parents picked the evacuees they liked. Scruffy children or groups of brothers and sisters were often passed over. Sometimes billeting officers had to take children round the local houses, trying to persuade unwilling families to take them.

▼ A luggage label showing their name and school was fixed to evacuees' clothes, in case they became lost.

LONDON COUNTY COUNCIL

Platt   Edith

○ STARCROSS SCHOOL
ST. PANCRAS. N.W.1
P.T.O.

Some evacuees were so homesick they returned home after only a few months, or even weeks. Others, though, were very happy with their new families, and stayed for several years. Children under five travelled with their mothers, who also needed billets. But there were often problems when mothers had to share someone else's house.

▲ A policeman checks a young evacuee's label at the station.

▼ This photograph shows evacuees registering with their new families in September 1939.

'I was the only child left in the school after the sorting. Apparently my lady hadn't arrived. I felt like the scrag end. But the door burst open and in she came, a golden-haired, beautifully dressed lady with the most gorgeous smile. 'Is this my little girl?' she said. I prayed, 'Yes please!' and it was my lady come for me at last.' [7]

Reluctant host families were sometimes cruel to their evacuees. But many foster families were very kind, and were terribly upset when their evacuees left them. They often stayed in touch for years afterwards. Some children even found it difficult to become part of their real family again, when they finally returned home.

'4 pm 'DIG FOR VICTORY'

Granny leads Mary and Tommy on a mid-afternoon ramble. As they chase her striding figure, they see a group of young women digging a field. They are all dressed alike, and singing. 'Hello,' one of them calls, 'Are you an evacuee – like me?' She walks over to them, smiling. There is mud on her overalls and smeared across her face.

▲ Posters asked people to 'Dig for Victory' by growing more crops.

Because food was so scarce, everyone had to help by growing more on the land. 'Land girls' in the Women's Land Army (WLA) had volunteered to leave their homes, a bit like evacuees, to live with families in farming areas. They helped farmers whose workers were fighting in the forces. Land girls worked a very hard 48-hour week, milking cows, digging ditches and picking crops. They often had to live in cottages without running water, electricity or gas. Most land girls had not done this kind of work before, but they enjoyed the comradeship of the Land Army.

◄ Land girls had to work long, hard hours to keep the country's farms running.

Many city children thrived on the freedom and fresh air of the countryside. Some of them had never been close to farm animals before. As you can see from the quote below, from a ten-year-old evacuee's essay, some of them did not even know what a cow was.

◀ Being close to farm animals was a magical experience for some evacuees.

'The cow has a tail, on which hangs a brush. With this it sends the flies away ... Under the cow hangs the milk. It is arranged for milking. When people milk, the milk comes and there is never an end to the supply. How the cow does it I have not yet realized.' [8]

People ate a healthier, more natural diet during the war, with plenty of fresh vegetables. The 'Dig for Victory' campaign encouraged everyone to grow food on allotments. People dug up tennis courts, cricket pitches, railway embankments and even the old moat of the Tower of London. The government said: 'We want not only the big man with the plough, but the little man with the spade.'

◀ People took a pride in how much food they could grow, even in small gardens. Anderson shelters were covered in earth, and many people used this soil to grow vegetables.

5pm 'CARELESS TALK'

'**H**alt! Who goes there?' Granny and the children are stopped at an army checkpoint. The soldiers say that a German plane has crashed nearby, and the pilot is missing. They ask to see Granny Robertson's identity card before they will let her through.

In wartime, there was widespread fear of enemy spies living undercover in Britain. They were believed to be sending messages to Germany by wireless. Spies were known as 'fifth columnists'. Everyone was under suspicion, especially people with foreign-sounding names. Identity cards were issued, so that people could prove who they were. You could be asked to produce your card at any time, especially when soldiers were searching for missing German pilots.

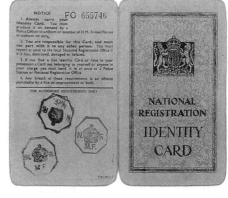

▲ An identity card from the war. It was important always to carry your card with you.

▼ This roadblock has been set up by members of the Home Guard.

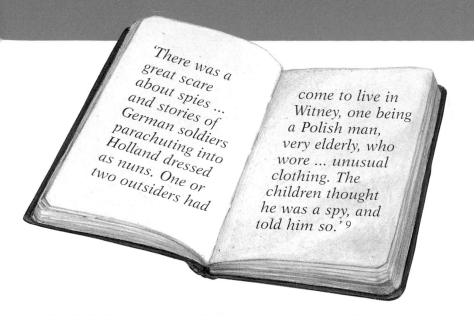

'There was a great scare about spies ... and stories of German soldiers parachuting into Holland dressed as nuns. One or two outsiders had come to live in Witney, one being a Polish man, very elderly, who wore ... unusual clothing. The children thought he was a spy, and told him so.'[9]

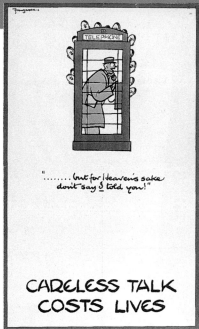

"........ but for Heaven's sake don't say I told you!"

CARELESS TALK COSTS LIVES

▲ This poster shows the German leader Adolf Hitler hiding round a telephone box. It warned people that German spies might be listening to their conversation.

Because of the fear of spies, posters warned people: 'Careless talk costs lives' and 'Walls have ears'. People were urged not to talk about anything that could help the enemy – for example, where soldiers were camped. If spies overheard this kind of information, and passed it to the enemy, British lives could be lost. In 1940, there was also a real danger that the German army would invade England. So, signposts were taken down to make it hard for enemy soldiers to find their way around.

◄ These men are removing the signposts near their town. Larger names, at railway stations for example, were painted out.

6pm AT THE PICTURES

Granny takes Mary to the pictures, to see a Laurel and Hardy film. They queue in the growing darkness because of the 'blackout' – no lights are allowed as they would give German planes an easy target for their bombs. The show starts with a Walt Disney cartoon, then news of the war, and finally the film.

By 1944, probably half the people in the country went to the pictures every week. There was no television, and the *Pathe News* was screened before every film to show the latest pictures of the war. The films of Stan Laurel and Oliver Hardy were popular with all ages. After 1939, their comedy adventures were given wartime themes to help people laugh at the problems of war.

◀ Laurel and Hardy, in their typical outfits.

▼ A 1943 cinema poster advertising Laurel and Hardy's adventures as air-raid wardens.

LAUREL & HARDY
ALARM

▶ There was a wireless like this one in every home. Radio broadcasts kept people informed about how the war was going.

Entertainment was especially important in wartime, when people were feeling sad and anxious. The 'wireless', or radio, was very popular. Most families listened to the news every single night, as announcers told them how many British and how many German planes had been lost. Comedies such as *ITMA* ('It's That Man Again') were also popular, while younger listeners enjoyed *Children's Hour*.

Popular songs helped people to share what the war meant to their lives. Children enjoyed singing songs such as *Run Rabbit, Hey Little Hen*, and *The White Cliffs of Dover*. Concerts and entertainments were put on in strange places, for example in buildings which had lost their roofs in the bombing. Evacuees sometimes helped to plan special entertainments for the whole of their street.

'There was no television – it was the wireless. At night sitting listening to the news was a very serious thing. I always remember my brother and I would start to laugh during the nine o'clock news and we would get put out in the lobby (hallway).' 10

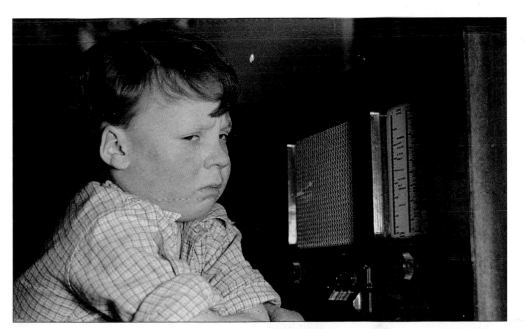

◀ This little boy is listening to the adventures of *Dick Barton – Special Agent*, who was a kind of wartime James Bond.

HOME GUARD

Grandpa Robertson has had to join his platoon tonight, to join in the search for the missing German pilot. The children stand in the road and watch as the Home Guard march past, their rifles on their shoulders. Grandpa looks smart in his uniform, with his sergeant's stripes. He gives the children a wink as he passes them.

▲ A book of Home Guard cartoons. Although people made jokes about the Home Guard, their role was actually very important.

The Home Guard was set up for men who were too old to join the forces, and those such as farmers and miners whose jobs were too important for them to leave. In May 1940, the first volunteers came forward to join what was then called the LDV (Local Defence Volunteers). Some 250,000 men joined in just twenty-four hours. The force was later renamed the Home Guard.

People made fun of the Home Guard. They called them 'Dad's Army' and said that LDV stood for 'Look, Duck and Vanish'. The Home Guard's image was not helped when the government issued them with old-fashioned pikes as weapons.

◀ Many older men who had fought in the First World War (1914–18) served in the Home Guard. This soldier is armed with a petrol bomb called a Molotov cocktail.

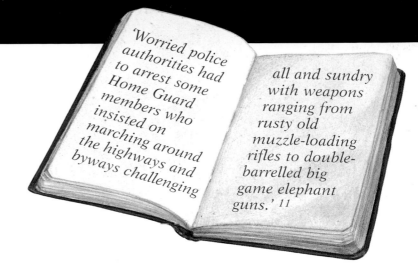

'Worried police authorities had to arrest some Home Guard members who insisted on marching around the highways and byways challenging all and sundry with weapons ranging from rusty old muzzle-loading rifles to double-barrelled big game elephant guns.' 11

◀ A Home Guard platoon in the months before they had proper uniforms.

The Home Guard's job was to protect the local area, especially the coastline, factories and airfields. At first, members had no proper uniforms or weapons. They made do with picks, pitchforks, golf clubs and old firearms borrowed from museums. They also made petrol bombs called Molotov cocktails, by filling old beer and wine bottles with an inflammable mixture of paraffin, petrol and tar.

During the day, members of the Home Guard did their normal jobs. In the evening, they trained and prepared for a German invasion. Home Guard commanders were ordered to sound the alarm by ringing church bells if the invasion started. On one occasion, the vicar of St Ives in Cornwall started an alert when he mistook the local fishing fleet for an enemy landing force.

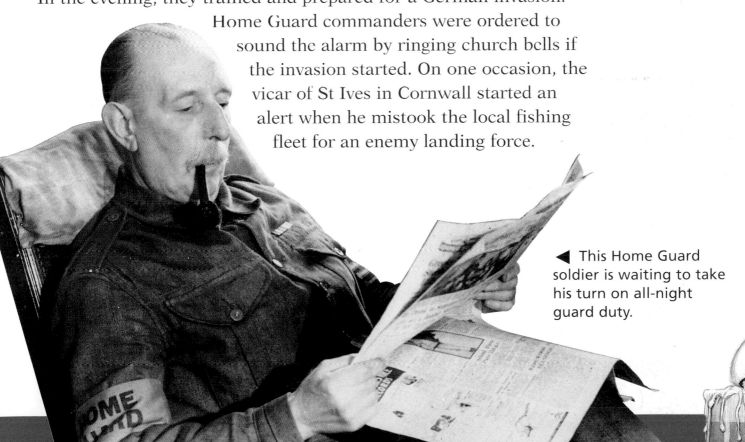

◀ This Home Guard soldier is waiting to take his turn on all-night guard duty.

10 pm FUN IN WARTIME

Mary was never allowed to stay up this late at home. She finishes her card home to mum, and watches Tommy and his friend march up and down with the toy guns Grandpa has given them. Grandpa tells them that the German pilot has been captured, and gives Tommy a piece of the crashed plane for his war collection.

▲ Paper was scarce, so children took it in turns to read precious copies of comics like *The Dandy, The Beano* and *Boy's Own*.

Being evacuated was very upsetting for children, but many settled down quickly. As adults always seemed so busy, children often had more freedom to play and explore. One girl said afterwards: 'It was strange – but it was good fun; we didn't realize the danger.'

Children enjoyed playing at soldiers, and reading comics full of war stories. But they also enjoyed helping with the real war. Older children carried messages, helped out in hospitals and filled up fire buckets. They also knitted scarves and blankets to send to the troops.

▶ For many children, the war was a time for exciting games.

◀ These children are proudly showing some of the things they have found, such as jagged pieces of bomb and shell cases. Large items might be handed in as scrap metal, but all the most interesting discoveries were kept in a safe place.

Boys and girls loved collecting anything to do with the war, such as buttons and badges, pieces of bomb cases and parts of aeroplanes. Groups of children toured the countryside on their bicycles, searching for souvenirs. Once, when a German plane was shot down near a village, the children had stripped it bare by the time the police arrived to guard it.

'We all had our own shrapnel collections, and it was great ... There would be pieces in the road. Some of it was really quite beautiful – it was all jagged but silvery-looking. It used to cut terribly.' 12

Children gathered souvenirs from crashed aeroplanes and bomb craters, then met in the playground to swap their latest finds. When they displayed their collections, they often added small flags to show which country's planes the pieces had been taken from.

◀ A war collection made by a boy called Jack Grice. He later joined the RAF, and lost his life fighting in Italy.

GLOSSARY

air-raid wardens   Officials appointed to organize people during air raids and blackouts.

allotment   A small piece of public land used for growing vegetables.

evacuee   Someone sent away from an area of danger to a safe place.

billeting officer   An official who helped to find homes for evacuees.

chamber pot   A potty kept under the bed.

checkpoint   A place, such as a roadblock, where people are stopped and their papers inspected.

crypt   A cellar or underground chamber.

identity card   A document which shows who someone is, where they are from and where they live.

incendiary bomb   A bomb designed to cause fires when it explodes.

inflammable   Easily set on fire.

logbook   A book in which a record of events or a trip is made.

nits   The nickname for head lice.

pikes   Old-fashioned weapons, with a metal spearhead on a long pole.

platoon   A unit of men in an army.

scrag end   A scrappy cut of meat that no one really wants.

siren   A machine used for making a loud air-raid warning.

spam   Tinned luncheon meat, made mainly from pork.

Spitfire   A famous British fighter plane.

Use a dictionary to find out more about the origins and meanings of some wartime words used in this book: Anderson shelter (p. 13); rations (p. 14); submarines (p. 14); land girls (p. 20); wireless (p. 22); blackout (p. 24); Home Guard (p. 26); shrapnel (p. 29).

BOOKS TO READ

Carrie's War by Nina Bawden (Puffin, 1993)
Daily Life in a Wartime House by Laura Wilson (Hamlyn, 1995)
Evacuation, The History Detective Investigates by Martin Parsons (Wayland, 1999)
Home in the Blitz by Marilyn Tolhurst (A & C Black, 1996)
Ration Book Recipes by Gill Corbishley (English Heritage, 1990)

Children can use this book to improve their literacy skills in the following ways:

✓ To compare the fictional opening paragraphs with the non-fiction text, noting differences in style and structure (Year 3, Term 1, non-fiction reading comprehension).

✓ To identify different types of text – biography, fiction, non-fiction, quotes, captions – by their content and lay-out (Year 4, Term 1, non-fiction reading comprehension).

✓ To use the footnoted quotes as an example of how authors record their sources (Year 5, Term 2, non-fiction reading comprehension).

✓ To explore the use of biography through the role of the historical character Mary (Year 6, Term 1, non-fiction reading comprehension and writing composition).

TIMELINE

February 1939	Anderson shelters are first delivered.
1 September 1939	German troops march into Poland.
1–3 September 1939	Mass evacuation of children in Britain, from cities to the countryside.
3 September 1939	At 11 am, Britain goes to war with Germany.
29 September 1939	Identity cards are issued.
January 1940	Food rationing begins.
14 May 1940	The first appeal for Local Defence Volunteers (Home Guard).
7 September 1940	The start of air raids on London (the Blitz). More children are evacuated.
19 September 1940	Hitler postpones plans to invade Britain.
October 1940	Princess Elizabeth (our Queen) broadcasts on *Children's Hour*.
January 1941	Fire-watching for German incendiary bombs is made compulsory.
March 1940	Jam, marmalade, syrup and treacle are rationed.
July 1942	Sweets are rationed.
6 June 1944	D-Day: British forces land in Europe.
12 June 1944	German V-1 bombs ('doodlebugs') launched at Britain: the last period of evacuation for children begins.
8 May 1945	VE Day (Victory in Europe).

INFORMATION ABOUT 'NEW ARRIVALS' ON PAGES 16–17

The five characters who appear elsewhere in the book are the teacher (p. 8) helping the new arrivals; the warden (p. 12) telling the grocer to tape up his windows; the grocer woman (p. 14) making deliveries by bicycle; the land girl (p. 20) with supplies; and the Home Guard soldier carrying a message. We can tell it is wartime because there is an air-raid warden and a ration queue; the car has its headlamps masked because of the blackout; the station sign is being painted out to confuse invading soldiers; the station windows have been taped up to prevent flying glass if a bomb lands; evacuees with labels and gas masks are arriving; there is a Home Guard soldier; and there are bins for recycling material.

SOURCES OF QUOTES

1. Evacuee's letter, private collection.
2. Rose Isserlis, from B. S. Johnson (ed.), *The Evacuees* (Gollancz, 1968).
3. Kate Eggleston in Jonathan Croall, *Don't You Know There's a War On* (Hutchinson, 1988).
4. Doreen Bridges, taped interview, author's collection.
5. Mary-Rose Murphy in Jonathan Croall, see above.
6. Kate Eggleston in Jonathan Croall, see above.
7. May Owen, from B.S. Johnson (ed.), *The Evacuees* (Gollancz, 1968).
8. *BBC News* (29.10.39): ten-year-old's essay, quoted in Susan Briggs, *Keep Smiling Through* (Book Club Associates, 1975).
9. John Dossett-Davies in Jonathan Croall, see above.
10. Mrs Anderson, taped interview.
11. Derek E. Johnson, *East Anglia at War* (Jarrolds, 1978).
12. Doreen Bridges, taped interview.

INDEX

Numbers in **bold** refer to pictures and captions.

aeroplanes **8**, 9, 10, 12, 13, 22, 24, 25, 29
air raids 9, 12, **12**, 13
air-raid shelters 12, 13, **13**, **21**
air-raid sirens 12, 13
air-raid wardens 10, 12, **12**, **13**, **24**
allotments 14
armed forces 8, 26

baths 6, 7, **7**
bed-wetting 7
billets 5, 6, **6**, 16, 18, 19
blackout 24
bombing 4, 5, 10, 12, **13**, 25

'careless talk' 22, 23, **23**
'cattle market' 18, 19, **19**
checkpoints 22, **22**
cinema 24, **24**
cities 4, 5
cod liver oil 7, **7**
collections 28, 29, **29**
comics 28, **28**
countryside 4, 5, 21

evacuation 4, 5, 6, **7**, 16, 18, **18**, 28

farming 20, 21, 26
fire-watching 12, **12**
food 14, **14**, 15, **15**, **17**, 20, 21
fundraising 9

games 28, **28**
gas masks **5**, 10, **10**, 11, **11**
Germany 5, 10, 12, 13, 14, 22, 23, 24, 26, 28, 29
government 5, **5**, 21, 26

head lice 6
health 6, 7, **7**, 21
Home Guard **22**, 26, **26**, 27, **27**
homesickness 4, 5, 19
host families 4, 6, 7, 16, 18, 19

identity cards 22, **22**
invasion 23, 27

labels **4**, **18**, **19**
Laurel and Hardy 24, **24**
locals 8, 9
London 5, 12

news 24, 25

pigs 15, **15**
posters 5, **5**, **15**, **20**, 23, **23**

radio 15, 22, 25, **25**
rationing 7, 14, **14**, 15, **15**, **17**

saving waste 15, **15**
schools **7**, 8, **8**, 9, **9**, 10, 11, **11**, 12, 13, **13**, **17**
shops 14, **14**, 15, **15**
signposts 23, **23**
songs 12, 25
spies 22, 23

teachers 8, **8**, 10, **11**

Women's Land Army 20, **20**